The Wisdom of Solomon

Timeless Insights on Justice, Faith, and Virtue

A Modern Translation

Adapted for the Contemporary Reader

King Solomon

Translated by Tim Zengerink

© **Copyright 2025**
All rights reserved.

It is not legal to reproduce, duplicate, or transmit any part of this document in either electronic means or in printed format. Recording of this publication is strictly prohibited and any storage of this document is not allowed unless with written permission from the publisher except for the use of brief quotations in a book review.

This book contains works of fiction. Any resemblance to persons living or dead, or places, events, or locations is purely coincidental.

Table Of Contents

Preface - Message to the Reader 1
Introduction 5
Chapter 1 13
Chapter 2 15
Chapter 3 18
Chapter 4 21
Chapter 5 24
Chapter 6 27
Chapter 7 30
Chapter 8 34
Chapter 9 37
Chapter 10 40
Chapter 11 43
Chapter 12 47
Chapter 13 51
Chapter 14 54
Chapter 15 58
Chapter 16 61
Chapter 17 65
Chapter 18 68
Chapter 19 71
Thank You for Reading 74

Preface - Message to the Reader

What If You Could Help Rebuild the Greatest Library in Human History?

Thousands of years ago, the Library of Alexandria stood as the crown jewel of human achievement — a sanctuary where the collected wisdom of every known civilization was gathered, preserved, and shared freely.

And then, it was lost.

Through fire, conquest, and the slow erosion of time, humanity lost not just books — but ideas, dreams, discoveries, and stories that could have changed the world forever.

Today, the Library of Alexandria lives again — and you are invited to be a part of its restoration.

Our mission is simple yet profound:

To rebuild the greatest library the world has ever known, and to translate all timeless works into every language and dialect, so that no seeker of knowledge is ever left behind again.

By joining our movement to rebuild the modern Library of Alexandria, you become part of an unprecedented mission:

- **Unlimited Access to the Greatest Audiobooks & eBooks Ever Written**

   Instantly explore thousands of legendary works—Plato, Shakespeare, Jane Austen, Leo Tolstoy, and countless more. All instantly available to read or listen, placing a complete literary universe at your fingertips.

- **Beautiful Paperback & Deluxe Editions at Printing Cost**

   Own any title as an elegant paperback, deluxe hardcover, or stunning collectible boxset—offered to you at true printing cost, delivered straight to your door. Build your personal Library of Alexandria, crafted for beauty, built for durability, and worthy of proud display.

- **Fresh Translations for Modern Readers—in Every Language & Dialect**

   Enjoy timeless masterpieces reimagined in clear, contemporary language—no more outdated phrases or obscure references. Alongside the original versions, we're tirelessly translating these classics into every language and dialect imaginable, ensuring accessibility and understanding across cultures and generations.

- **Join a Global Renaissance of Literature & Knowledge**

    You directly support expanding our library, publishing deluxe editions at true cost, translating works into all global languages, and bringing humanity's greatest stories to people everywhere. By joining today, you're not just preserving a legacy of masterpieces; you set in motion a powerful wave of literary accessibility.

Become a Torchbearer of Knowledge.

Join us for free now at **LibraryofAlexandria.com**

Together, we will ensure that the light of human wisdom never fades again.

With gratitude and a shared love of knowledge,

The Modern Library of Alexandria Team

Visit:

www.libraryofalexandria.com

Or scan the code below:

Introduction

Timeless Insights on Justice, Faith, and Virtue

Throughout history, humanity has continually sought wisdom—an enduring quest for deeper understanding, ethical guidance, and insights into life's greatest mysteries. Among the rich traditions of ancient wisdom literature, one text stands out prominently: The Wisdom of Solomon. Attributed to the renowned King Solomon, legendary for his profound wisdom and insightful judgment, this work transcends its historical origins to offer timeless reflections on morality, justice, faith, and the pursuit of a meaningful life.

Believed by tradition to be composed by King Solomon himself, celebrated across numerous cultures for his legendary wisdom, this profound text emerged during a formative period of Jewish thought, deeply influencing subsequent religious and philosophical traditions. Although modern scholarship often situates its composition within the Hellenistic period (approximately first century BCE), its attribution to

Solomon symbolizes the epitome of wisdom, lending significant authority and gravitas to its teachings.

Historical and Cultural Context

The Wisdom of Solomon is part of a collection of ancient texts known as the Wisdom Literature, which also includes Proverbs, Ecclesiastes, and Job. These texts emerged from a vibrant intellectual and spiritual milieu, blending Hebrew religious thought with the philosophical and ethical traditions of surrounding cultures, notably Greek philosophy. The synthesis of Jewish spirituality with Hellenistic intellectual rigor makes The Wisdom of Solomon uniquely compelling and universally relevant.

This text was likely written in Greek within the Jewish diaspora community of Alexandria, Egypt—a center of learning and intellectual exchange between Jewish, Greek, and Egyptian cultures. This rich cultural context profoundly influenced its content, characterized by philosophical sophistication, poetic elegance, and deeply spiritual insight. The Wisdom of Solomon thus represents not only a powerful spiritual text but also a significant historical artifact, reflecting the complex interplay of diverse traditions and ideas.

Major Themes Explored

At its core, The Wisdom of Solomon explores fundamental themes essential for living a righteous, fulfilling, and spiritually aware life. These themes, timeless and universal, resonate deeply with contemporary readers seeking moral clarity, ethical leadership, and spiritual depth.

1. The Pursuit and Nature of Wisdom

Central to this work is the theme of wisdom itself—its nature, pursuit, and profound significance for human life. Wisdom is presented not merely as intellectual knowledge but as deep spiritual understanding rooted in reverence for the divine. Solomon emphasizes wisdom's transformative power, guiding individuals toward righteousness, justice, and a closer relationship with God. This pursuit of wisdom is depicted as an active, ongoing journey essential for personal and communal flourishing.

2. Divine Justice and Human Morality

Another foundational theme in The Wisdom of Solomon is divine justice, particularly how it intersects with human morality. The text explores the nature of justice, emphasizing fairness, integrity, and righteousness as divine attributes mirrored by ethical human conduct. Solomon highlights the eventual triumph of justice over injustice, assuring readers of divine providence and encouraging steadfastness in virtue even amidst adversity.

3. Faith and Trust in the Divine

Faith emerges as a critical pillar throughout Solomon's reflections. Readers are encouraged to cultivate deep trust and reliance on the divine, recognizing God's wisdom, justice, and providential care. Solomon assures that true wisdom begins with faith—a reverent acknowledgment of God's sovereignty and goodness. This trust empowers individuals to navigate life's uncertainties with resilience, confidence, and spiritual clarity.

4. Ethical Leadership and Virtuous Living

Embedded in Solomon's teachings are profound insights into ethical leadership and virtuous living. He advocates for leadership grounded in justice, compassion, humility, and moral integrity, underscoring the significant responsibilities borne by leaders in shaping ethical communities. Solomon's vision extends to individual conduct, urging readers to embody virtues such as honesty, kindness, humility, and courage in their daily lives.

The Structure and Style of the Text

The Wisdom of Solomon is characterized by poetic eloquence, philosophical depth, and vivid imagery, rendering its profound teachings accessible and inspiring. Its structured chapters blend poetry, prose, and prayerful meditation, offering a multifaceted exploration of wisdom's transformative power. The elegant language and thoughtful composition make the text not only spiritually enriching but aesthetically compelling, inviting readers into profound contemplation and reflection.

Relevance for Today's World

In today's complex and often turbulent world, the teachings of The Wisdom of Solomon resonate powerfully, offering timeless guidance for ethical living, spiritual depth, and moral clarity. Contemporary readers—whether spiritual seekers, ethical leaders, scholars, or individuals striving for personal growth—find within its pages valuable insights applicable to modern challenges.

- Navigating Moral Complexity: Solomon's clear ethical guidelines and emphasis on justice and integrity help readers address contemporary moral

dilemmas, fostering discernment, empathy, and principled decision-making.
- Cultivating Spiritual Awareness: The emphasis on wisdom as spiritual insight and connection to the divine resonates deeply with individuals seeking spiritual enrichment, deeper meaning, and authentic relationships with the divine.
- Encouraging Virtuous Leadership: Solomon's teachings on leadership emphasize essential qualities—justice, humility, compassion—that remain critically important today, inspiring contemporary leaders in various fields.

Why This Modern Translation Matters

This modern translation of The Wisdom of Solomon is carefully crafted to make its profound teachings accessible and relevant for contemporary readers. By preserving the poetic beauty and spiritual depth of the original text while presenting it in clear, relatable language, this adaptation bridges ancient wisdom and modern experience. It ensures readers from diverse backgrounds can deeply engage with these timeless insights, applying them meaningfully within their lives and communities.

Inviting Personal and Spiritual Reflection

Engaging with The Wisdom of Solomon is more than an academic or historical exercise; it is an invitation into deep personal and spiritual reflection. Each chapter, verse, and poetic expression encourages readers to examine their own lives, beliefs, and actions critically and authentically.

As you journey through this text, take time to reflect upon its teachings, considering how they relate to your personal experiences, ethical challenges, spiritual questions, and aspirations. Allow Solomon's timeless wisdom to inspire, challenge, and guide you toward greater clarity, purpose, and spiritual fulfillment.

Conclusion: Embark on Your Journey into Wisdom

The Wisdom of Solomon stands as an enduring beacon of insight, spiritual depth, and ethical guidance, illuminating pathways toward justice, faith, virtue, and wisdom. Its teachings transcend historical boundaries, offering profound insights that enrich personal and communal life today.

Translated by Tim Zengerink

May your exploration of this transformative text deepen your understanding, inspire spiritual growth, and empower you to live a life characterized by integrity, wisdom, and purpose. Begin your journey into Solomon's timeless wisdom, discovering insights that will profoundly shape your faith, character, and vision for a meaningful life.

Chapter 1

Love what is right, all of you who lead and judge others. Keep your thoughts pure and seek the Lord with a sincere heart. He makes Himself known to those who trust Him and allows Himself to be found by those who truly want to understand Him.

Wrong thinking leads people away from God, and those who try to challenge Him will be proven foolish. Wisdom cannot stay with someone who chooses evil, and it cannot live in a body controlled by sin.

A spirit that is holy and disciplined avoids lies, rejects foolish thinking, and stays far from wrongdoing. Wisdom is a gift that helps people, but it does not ignore those who speak against God. He sees what is in every heart and knows our deepest thoughts.

The Spirit of the Lord fills the whole world, holds everything together, and hears every word spoken. No one who speaks dishonestly can hide, and justice will not let them go unpunished.

Wicked people will be exposed by their actions, and the words they speak will reach God, revealing their wrongdoing. Nothing is truly hidden—every whisper is heard, and no secret escapes His attention.

Be careful not to complain needlessly or speak badly about others. Every word matters, and lies can destroy a soul. Do not bring harm upon yourself by choosing the wrong path, and do not invite destruction through your actions.

God did not create death, and He does not take pleasure in seeing people suffer. Everything He made was meant to thrive, and the forces of nature were created without destruction in them. Righteousness leads to eternal life.

But the wicked bring death upon themselves through their choices and words. They treat it like a friend, wasting their lives and forming a bond with it. Through their actions, they show that they belong to its power.

Chapter 2

Their way of thinking was completely wrong, yet they convinced themselves:

"Life is short and full of trouble. There's no way to escape death, and no one has ever come back from the grave.

We were born by accident, and when we die, it will be as if we never existed. Our breath disappears like smoke, and our thoughts are just tiny sparks that flicker for a moment.

When that spark dies out, our bodies turn to dust, and our spirits vanish like the wind.

As time passes, people will forget our names, and everything we did will be erased. Our lives will disappear like a passing cloud or vanish like mist under the heat of the sun.

Our time on earth is like a shadow that quickly fades, and nothing can stop the end from coming.

So, let's enjoy life while we can. Let's take in all the pleasures of the world while we're still young.

We'll drink the finest wine and enjoy the sweetest perfumes. We won't miss a single moment to admire the beauty of spring.

We'll make ourselves crowns of flowers before they wilt and make sure we experience every desire we have.

We'll leave our mark wherever we go because this is what we deserve—this is the life we were meant to live.

Let's take advantage of the weak, show no kindness to widows, and ignore the wisdom of the elderly.

Only power matters—if you're weak, you're useless.

Let's go after the righteous man because he's a problem for us. He challenges our actions, calls us lawbreakers, and points out that we don't even follow our own rules.

He claims to know God and even calls himself a child of the Lord.

He looks down on us and refuses to live as we do, saying our ways are wrong. He insists that good people will have a happy ending and proudly declares that God is his father.

Let's test him to see if he's telling the truth. Let's find out what happens to him in the end.

If he really is a child of God, then God will protect him and keep him from harm.

Let's insult him and make him suffer to see how patient and humble he really is.

Let's give him a shameful death and see if God saves him, just like he claims."

This is how they thought, but they were completely wrong. Their own evil blinded them.

They didn't understand God's ways or believe in the rewards of living a good life. They had no idea what was in store for those who live with honesty and faith.

God created people to live forever and made them in His own image.

But death entered the world because of the devil's jealousy, and only those who follow him will experience it.

Chapter 3

The souls of good and faithful people are safe with God, and nothing can harm them. To those who don't understand, their death might look like a terrible loss. It may seem like their lives ended in failure, but the truth is—they are at peace.

Even if it looks like they suffered, their future is full of hope because they will live forever. After going through a short time of testing, they will receive amazing rewards. God examined them and saw that they were worthy of Him.

He purified them, just like gold is refined in fire, and accepted them as a perfect offering. When their reward comes, they will shine brightly and move like sparks through dry grass.

They will rule over nations and lead people, and the Lord will always be their King.

Those who trust in Him will understand the truth, and those who remain loyal will live with Him in love, because He shows kindness and mercy to those He has chosen.

But those who live without God will be judged for their actions and thoughts. They turned away from what is right and refused to follow the Lord.

People who reject wisdom and discipline bring misery upon themselves. Their hopes are empty, their hard work leads to nothing, and everything they try to accomplish will fail.

Their wives will act foolishly, their children will follow in their wicked ways, and their entire family line will be ruined.

On the other hand, a woman who has done no wrong, even if she has no children, is blessed. She will be joyful when God judges all people and gives out His rewards.

A man who stays faithful, avoids sin, and keeps his heart pure before the Lord is also blessed. He will receive great rewards and a joyful place among God's people.

Doing what is right will always bring honor, and a life built on wisdom will never fall apart.

But children born from unfaithful relationships will struggle. The children of sin will eventually fade away.

Even if they live a long time, they will not be respected, and their old age will bring them no dignity.

If they die young, they will have no hope or comfort when they stand before God.

A family that comes from evil and dishonesty will always face sorrow and hardship.

Chapter 4

It is far better to live a good and honorable life, even without children, because doing what is right brings lasting value. A good life is remembered by both God and people. It inspires others while it lasts, and when it is gone, people long for it to return. It moves through time with honor, achieving rewards that are pure and everlasting.

But the many descendants of wicked people bring no real benefit. The children of those who live without goodness will not take root or last. Even if they seem to grow for a little while, they will be weak and easily blown away like dust in the wind. Strong storms will rip them from the ground completely.

Their branches will snap before they fully grow, and their fruit will be worthless—unfit to eat or use for anything good. Children born from sinful acts will stand as proof of their parents' wrongdoings when the time comes for judgment.

But a good person, even if they die young, will find peace. True honor in life isn't about how many years a person lives or how much time passes. Instead, wisdom is like gray hair for the soul, and a pure life is just as valuable as growing old.

A person who pleases God is deeply loved by Him. When they live among those who do wrong, God takes them away to protect them from harm.

They are removed before evil can corrupt their heart or before lies can lead them astray. Wickedness has a way of darkening even the brightest soul, and uncontrolled desires can mislead even the purest heart.

A life that reaches its purpose quickly is just as meaningful as a long one. The soul of a good person brings joy to the Lord, so He takes them away from the corruption around them.

Those who see this happening don't understand. They don't realize that God shows love and mercy to those He has chosen and that He watches over those who live in holiness.

Even after death, a good person's life will stand as a reminder to those who live in wickedness. A young person who lives with wisdom and goodness will reveal the flaws of an old person who has spent their years doing wrong.

The ungodly will see the end of a wise person's life but won't understand what God had planned or why He protected them.

They will see, but instead of learning from it, they will be filled with resentment. And just as they rejected wisdom, the Lord will turn away from them.

In the end, they will be nothing but dishonored bodies, a disgrace among the dead.

God will bring them down, leaving them speechless and trembling. Their lives will fall apart, leaving them in misery, and their names will soon be forgotten.

When the time comes for their sins to be counted, fear will consume them. Their own actions will be the proof against them, standing as witnesses to all the wrong they have done.

Chapter 5

The good and faithful will stand tall and unshaken in front of those who once mistreated them and thought they were worthless. When their enemies see them, they will be filled with fear and shock, completely stunned by the unexpected sight of their victory.

Full of regret, they will whisper to each other, saying, "Is this really the person we used to mock? The one we laughed at and thought was foolish? We believed their life had no meaning and that their death was a disgrace.

But now, look at them! How did they become part of God's people? How are they counted among those who are holy?

We were the ones who were blind and foolish. We strayed far from the truth. We never found the light of righteousness, and we lived without real direction.

Instead of following what was right, we chased after destruction. We ignored the ways of the Lord and spent our lives lost and wandering.

What did we gain from our pride? What good did our wealth and bragging bring us? Nothing. Everything we built disappeared in an instant, like a shadow passing by or a gust of wind that leaves no trace.

It's like a ship sailing through rough waters—once it's gone, there's no sign it was ever there, no mark left on the waves.

Or like a bird flying across the sky—the air moves for a moment as its wings pass through, but once it's gone, there's no proof it was ever there.

Or like an arrow shot from a bow—the air parts briefly, but it quickly comes back together, leaving no sign of the arrow's flight.

In the same way, we lived our lives and disappeared without a trace. We left nothing good behind because we were consumed by our own wrongdoings."

The hopes of the wicked are weak and fragile—like dust blown away by the wind, or foam that disappears in a storm. Their memories fade like smoke drifting in the air or like a visitor who stays only for a short while before being forgotten.

But those who have lived righteously will live forever, receiving their reward from the Lord Himself. The Most High will care for them and bless them with eternal life.

They will be crowned with glory, and the Lord will personally place a royal crown upon their heads. He will protect them and cover them with His power.

God will prepare for battle, wrapping Himself in passion like armor, using all of creation as His weapon to bring justice against His enemies.

Righteousness will be His chest plate, and fairness will be His helmet.

He will hold holiness as a shield and sharpen His burning anger like a sword.

All of creation will join Him in the fight, standing with Him against those who oppose Him.

Lightning bolts will strike with perfect aim, flashing down like arrows fired from a skilled archer's bow.

Hailstones will fall like deadly weapons, crashing down with unstoppable force. The waters of the sea will rise up in fury, and rivers will overflow, sweeping away His enemies.

A powerful wind will come like a storm, scattering them and leaving nothing behind.

Their wickedness will bring destruction upon the earth, and their corruption will cause even the mightiest thrones to collapse.

Chapter 6

Listen, kings, and pay attention. Listen carefully, rulers of the earth. Hear this, you who govern many people and take pride in ruling over countless nations.

Your power comes from the Lord, and your authority is given by the Most High. One day, He will hold you accountable for how you used it and ask about the choices you made.

You were meant to lead with fairness, but instead, you failed to bring justice and did not follow God's ways.

Because of this, He will judge you swiftly and without hesitation. Those in power will face a stricter judgment.

Ordinary people may find mercy and forgiveness, but leaders will be held to a higher standard and judged more seriously.

The Lord of all does not show favoritism. He is not influenced by status or impressed by power because He created both the mighty and the weak, and He cares for everyone equally.

But those who have been given greater responsibility will face greater scrutiny.

These words are for you, rulers, so that you may learn wisdom and stay on the right path.

Those who respect what is holy will be blessed, and those who seek wisdom will learn how to defend what is right.

Desire wisdom and treasure her, rulers, and she will guide you.

Wisdom shines brightly and never fails. She is easy to find for those who love her and reveals herself to those who seek her.

She makes herself known to those who long for her and eagerly comes to those who desire her.

Anyone who searches for wisdom early in the morning will find her waiting at their doorstep, ready to be embraced.

Thinking about wisdom brings complete understanding, and staying focused on her removes all worries.

Wisdom searches for those who are worthy of her. She shows herself to them and gently guides their every choice.

The first step toward wisdom is wanting to learn, and the love of learning leads to a desire for understanding.

Loving wisdom means following her ways, and keeping her ways leads to eternal life.

Eternal life brings a person closer to God.

So, the pursuit of wisdom leads to the path of a lasting kingdom.

If you desire power and authority, rulers of the earth, seek wisdom, and you will rule wisely forever.

I will reveal what wisdom is and where she comes from. I will not keep her secrets hidden but will share her knowledge for all to understand. I will not withhold the truth.

I refuse to let jealousy consume me because envy cannot exist alongside wisdom.

A nation guided by wisdom brings safety to the world, and a wise leader provides stability to his people.

So listen closely to my words, accept this teaching, and you will gain great wisdom.

Chapter 7

I am human, just like everyone else—a descendant of the first person formed from the earth. My body took shape over ten months in my mother's womb, nourished by her blood, created through human life and the bond of marriage.

When I was born, I breathed the same air as everyone else and rested on the same ground. Like all newborns, I cried out with my first voice. I was cared for, wrapped in soft cloth, and nurtured.

No king is born differently, for every person enters life in the same way and leaves it in the same way.

Knowing this, I prayed, and I was given understanding. I asked, and wisdom was given to me.

I valued her more than power and riches, and wealth meant nothing to me compared to her.

I didn't see her as less important than the most valuable gems, because next to her, gold is like a handful of dust, and silver is no more than clay.

I loved her more than health and beauty and chose her over even the brightest light because her glow never fades.

With her came every good thing, and in her hands were endless treasures.

I rejoiced in them all because wisdom guided them, though at first, I didn't realize she was the source of them all.

I gained wisdom honestly and now share what I've learned freely, hiding nothing from others.

She is an endless treasure for those who embrace her, and through her, they build a close relationship with God, who praises them for the gifts they share through wisdom.

May God grant me the ability to speak wisely and think thoughts that reflect the wisdom I've been given, for He leads wisdom and corrects those who seek understanding.

Both we and our words are in His hands, as well as all knowledge and the ability to create and build.

He gave me deep understanding of the universe and how everything in it works together.

I know how time unfolds—the past, present, and future—the changes of the seasons, and the cycles of the years.

I have learned about the movement of stars, the nature of living creatures, the instincts of wild animals, the force of the wind, and the thoughts in human hearts.

I understand the variety of plants and the hidden powers of their roots.

I have been taught all things, both seen and unseen, because wisdom, the designer of all creation, has been my teacher.

Wisdom is a spirit that is intelligent, holy, one of a kind, subtle, free-moving, clear in speech, pure, strong, and always seeking what is good.

She is sharp, unhindered, kind, devoted to people, steady, unwavering, free from worry, powerful, all-seeing, and able to move through all minds that are wise, pure, and open.

She moves more smoothly than anything else and touches everything because of her purity.

She is the breath of God's power, a shining reflection of His glory. Nothing corrupt can enter her.

She is the light of eternity, a perfect mirror of God's work, and an image of His goodness.

Though she is one, she can do all things. She remains unchanged while renewing all things. She enters the hearts of good people in every generation, making them close to God and guiding them as His messengers.

God loves no one more than those who welcome wisdom into their lives.

She is more beautiful than the sun and shines brighter than all the stars. Her light is greater than even the brightest day.

For while daylight fades into night, wisdom can never be overcome by darkness.

Chapter 8

Her wisdom reaches across the entire universe, guiding everything with perfect order and balance. From a young age, I loved her deeply and longed to make her my companion. Her beauty and goodness completely captivated me.

She shows her greatness by staying close to God, and He treasures her above all things. She has a deep understanding of God and works in perfect harmony with His plans.

If wealth is something to be desired, then what could be richer than wisdom, which creates all things? If understanding is what we seek, who is wiser than the one who designed the universe?

If someone values goodness, wisdom produces it in abundance. She teaches self-control, insight, fairness, and courage—the most important qualities anyone can have.

If experience is what matters, wisdom holds knowledge of the past and can reveal what is to come. She understands every language, explains mysteries, and reveals hidden truths. She knows how the seasons change and can predict events before they happen.

This is why I chose to make her my guide, knowing she would lead me with wisdom and support me through every challenge and difficulty.

With her by my side, I will earn honor among great crowds and gain the respect of elders, even while I am still young.

People will recognize my sound judgment and respect me in the presence of rulers.

When I remain silent, others will wait eagerly for my words. When I begin to speak, they will listen closely. If I continue, they will be drawn in, holding back their own words just to hear more.

With wisdom, I will achieve a lasting legacy, and my name will be remembered for generations.

I will have the power to govern nations and lead many people.

Even the strongest rulers will hear my name and feel awe. Among the people, I will be celebrated for my kindness and praised for my courage in times of trouble.

And when I return home, wisdom will bring me peace. Conversations with her are never dull, and her presence fills life with joy and satisfaction.

As I thought about all of this—how wisdom leads to a fulfilling life, how her friendship brings true happiness, how her efforts create lasting success, how she grants deep understanding, and how her words bring honor—I decided I had to seek her with all my heart.

Even as a child, I had a curious mind and a good heart.

Or maybe, because I tried to be good, I was given the gift of a pure soul.

But I realized that wisdom could not truly be mine unless God gave her to me. I understood that this kind of insight comes only from Him.

So, I turned my heart toward God, and with complete sincerity, I prayed to Him and begged for His guidance.

Chapter 9

O Lord, God of my ancestors, the source of all
 mercy,
You spoke the world into existence with just Your
 word.
With Your wisdom,
You created humanity,
Giving them the responsibility to care for Your
 creation,
To lead with justice and truth,
And to judge fairly with honest and pure hearts.

Please give me wisdom, the one who stands beside
 You.
Do not leave me out from among Your faithful
 servants.
I am Your servant, the child of Your handmaid,
A mortal being, weak and short-lived,
Lacking full understanding of justice and truth.

Even if a person is seen as perfect,
Without Your wisdom, they are nothing.
You have chosen me to lead Your people,
To guide the sons and daughters of Israel.

Translated by Tim Zengerink

You have commanded me to build a sacred temple
    on Your holy mountain,
An altar in the city where You dwell,
A reflection of the holy place You established long
    ago.

Wisdom is with You and knows all that You do.
She was there when You created the world.
She understands what pleases You
And what is right according to Your commands.

Send her down from Your holy dwelling,
Let her come from Your glorious throne.
Let her be by my side to guide me,
So that I may do what is right in Your eyes.

She knows all things and leads with great wisdom.
She will show me the right way to act
And protect me with her shining light.
With her, my actions will be just,
I will lead Your people with fairness,
And I will be worthy to continue my father's work.

Who can truly understand Your plans, O God?
Who can know what You desire?
Human thoughts are fragile,
And our plans often fail.

Our bodies weigh down our souls,
And our earthly worries cloud our minds.
We struggle to understand even the things close to us,
So how can we possibly understand the things of heaven?
Who could know Your will unless You give them wisdom
And send Your Holy Spirit from above?

Wisdom is the one who guides people on earth,
Through her, we learn what pleases You,
And through her, we are saved.

Chapter 10

Wisdom protected the first father of the world, watching over him until the end. Though he was created alone, wisdom saved him from his mistakes and gave him the power to rule over all creation.

But when a wicked man turned away from wisdom in anger, he brought destruction upon himself. His rage led him to commit the worst sin—killing his own brother.

When the world was filled with evil, and a great flood came, wisdom stepped in again. She guided the one righteous man who was saved in a small wooden ark.

Later, when people united in rebellion and were scattered in confusion, wisdom recognized the righteous man among them. She kept him pure before God and gave him strength when he felt the pain of losing his child.

When the ungodly faced destruction, wisdom rescued the one righteous man who escaped the fiery judgment that fell on five sinful cities.

Their sin is still remembered today—through the smoking wasteland that remains, the fruit that looks good but never ripens, and the pillar of salt standing as a reminder of their disbelief.

By rejecting wisdom, they lost all sense of what is good and left behind a lasting sign of their foolishness. Their downfall serves as a warning for all time.

But wisdom always saves those who trust in her and rescues them from harm.

When a righteous man fled from his brother's anger, wisdom guided him in the right direction. She taught him God's ways and helped him understand sacred truths. She blessed his hard work and made his efforts successful.

When greed led others to mistreat him, wisdom stood by his side and turned his struggles into success.

She protected him from his enemies, ruined the plans of those who tried to harm him, and proved that righteousness is stronger than any earthly power.

When a good man was sold into slavery, wisdom never left him. She kept him from sin, stayed with him even in the darkness of the prison, and gave him strength through his chains.

She remained with him until he was freed and brought to a throne, giving him power over those who had once oppressed him. She exposed the lies of his enemies and gave him lasting honor.

Wisdom saved an innocent people, rescuing a holy generation from the hands of those who enslaved them.

She entered the heart of a faithful servant of God, giving him the courage to stand against mighty kings with signs and miracles.

She rewarded the righteous, led them on an incredible journey, protected them during the day, and became a pillar of fire to guide them at night.

She safely brought them across the Red Sea and through the deep waters.

But she destroyed their enemies, drowning them in the sea.

The righteous took the wealth of the wicked and lifted their voices in praise, honoring Your holy name, Lord. They sang songs to celebrate Your mighty hand, which fought for them.

For wisdom gave speech to those who could not speak and even gave infants the ability to speak clearly.

Chapter 11

Wisdom guided a holy prophet, making sure everything he did was successful. She led the people safely through a dry and empty desert, where they set up camp in unfamiliar land.

They stood strong against their enemies and pushed back those who tried to harm them.

When they became thirsty, they cried out to You, and You answered by bringing water from a solid rock. Streams flowed from stone, giving them life.

What had been a punishment for their enemies became a blessing for Your people in their time of need.

While their enemies suffered as rivers turned into thick, clotted blood—punishment for ordering the deaths of infants—You gave Your people an endless supply of fresh water, more than they ever expected.

By letting them experience thirst, You showed them how severe their enemies' punishment really was.

When Your people were tested, You corrected them gently with kindness and mercy. But the ungodly faced harsh judgment, suffering greatly.

You disciplined Your people like a loving father, but You punished their enemies like a strict judge handing down a sentence.

No matter where their enemies were—near or far—they all suffered the same.

They grieved and groaned as they remembered the past.

When they saw how their suffering had turned into a blessing for others, they started to understand Your power.

They no longer mocked the one they had once rejected.

In the end, they were filled with awe. Their thirst was nothing like that of the righteous.

Because of their foolishness in worshiping useless animals and lowly creatures, You sent swarms of mindless beasts to punish them.

Through this, You taught them that people are often punished by the very things they sin with.

Your mighty hand, which shaped the world from nothing, was not limited in its power. You could have sent fierce bears, roaring lions, or newly created, unknown beasts filled with rage—breathing fire, blowing smoke, and flashing sparks from their eyes.

These creatures could have destroyed through sheer violence, but their presence alone would have been terrifying.

Yet, You didn't need them. With just a single breath, You could have wiped them out.

Justice would have chased them down, scattering them like dust in the wind with the power of Your might.

But You, in Your wisdom, balance all things perfectly, measuring them with precision.

Your strength is unshakable and cannot be challenged. Who could stand against the power of Your arm?

To You, the entire world is as small as a grain of sand on a scale or a drop of morning dew on the ground.

Yet, despite all Your power, You show mercy to everything, because You can do all things.

Instead of destroying people for their sins, You give them time to turn back to You.

You love everything You have made and hate nothing, for if You despised it, it wouldn't even exist.

Translated by Tim Zengerink

If You had not wanted it to be, how could anything have survived? How could anything continue without Your command?

You protect all living things because they belong to You, O Lord, the One who loves all life.

Chapter 12

Your perfect spirit is present in everything.

You gently correct those who go astray, reminding them of their mistakes so they can turn away from evil and believe in You, Lord.

The people who first lived in Your sacred land did terrible things. They practiced magic, performed unholy rituals, and had no mercy.

They sacrificed their own children, ate human flesh and blood, and made alliances based on evil. They even killed innocent infants.

You commanded their destruction through our ancestors so that the land, which is precious to You, could be given to people who would honor and serve You.

Still, You treated even these wicked people with some mercy, recognizing them as human beings. Instead of wiping them out all at once, You sent hornets to slowly drive them away.

It wasn't because You lacked the power to destroy them instantly. With one word, You could have sent mighty warriors or fierce creatures to wipe them out.

But You judged them gradually, giving them a chance to change, even though You knew their hearts were corrupt from the start and unlikely to turn to You.

From the beginning, they were destined for destruction. You didn't ignore their sins out of fear of anyone.

Who could question Your actions and ask, "Why did You do this?"

Who could argue against Your decisions or claim You were unfair for removing nations that had become unworthy?

Who could defend such evil people before You?

There is no other god besides You, the one who cares for all creation. No one can say that Your judgments are unjust.

No king or ruler can stand against You or overturn what You decide.

You are just and rule everything with fairness, never punishing someone who doesn't deserve it.

Your strength is the foundation of Your justice, and because You have complete authority, You are patient with us.

When people doubt Your power, You show them Your strength and humble those who question You.

Yet, even with all Your power, You judge with kindness and lead with great patience, acting at the time You choose.

Through this, You taught Your people that true justice should also come with kindness.

You gave Your children hope, showing them that You always provide a chance to repent when they sin.

If You were patient with the enemies of Your people—those who deserved destruction—giving them time to turn from evil,

how much more carefully do You judge Your own children, to whom You made promises through their ancestors?

When You discipline us, You are even harsher with our enemies, teaching us to recognize Your goodness when we judge and to seek Your mercy when we are judged.

The wicked, who lived foolishly, were punished through their own sinful ways.

They strayed far from the truth, worshiping animals as gods—creatures even their enemies found shameful. They were misled and acted like senseless children.

So, You judged them in a way that matched their own foolishness, treating them as they behaved—like ignorant children.

Those who ignored Your gentle warnings eventually faced the full punishment they deserved.

Through the very creatures they worshiped as gods, they suffered, and in their pain, they finally recognized the one true God they had once rejected.

In the end, their guilt was undeniable, and their punishment was just.

Chapter 13

All those who did not understand God were naturally unwise. They failed to recognize the One who created everything, even though His existence was clear in the world around them. They could not see the Creator through the beauty of His works.

Instead, they believed that fire, wind, the air, the stars, the raging seas, or the bright lights in the sky were gods that ruled over the earth.

If they thought these things were gods because of how beautiful they were, they should have realized that the One who created them must be even greater, for He is the true source of beauty.

And if they were amazed by the power of nature, they should have understood that the Creator is far mightier.

The greatness and beauty of creation give us a glimpse of the One who made them all.

Still, these people deserve only some blame, for perhaps they were searching for God and got lost along the way.

They carefully studied His creation, using their senses to admire the wonders of the world.

But even then, they have no excuse.

If they had enough intelligence to study the universe and its mysteries, how did they fail to find the One who created it all?

Instead, they placed their trust in lifeless things, calling them gods—objects made by human hands from gold and silver, shaped to look like animals or carved from stone by ancient craftsmen.

For example, a woodworker cuts down a tree that is easy to shape. He strips off its bark and carves it into something useful for his daily life.

The leftover wood he burns to cook his meals and satisfy his hunger.

Then, using a rough piece of wood that is full of knots, he carves it with little effort, shaping it with the skills he has learned in his free time. He might make it look like a person or even a small animal. He paints it red, covering its flaws with dye.

After finishing, he finds a place for it, fixing it to a wall and securing it with iron so that it won't fall over, knowing it is too weak to stand on its own.

Even though he knows it is just a piece of wood, he prays to it for blessings on his home, his marriage, and his children.

He asks a lifeless object to give him good health. He seeks life from something that is dead.

He begs for help from something that has no understanding.

For a safe journey, he looks for guidance from something that cannot take a single step.

And for success in his work and business, he puts his trust in something with hands that cannot move.

Chapter 14

Someone preparing to sail across dangerous seas puts their trust in a piece of wood, even though the wood itself is weaker than the ship that carries them.

Ships were created because people wanted to make money, and it was human skill and wisdom that shaped them.

But, O Father, it is You who truly guides their journey. You created paths in the sea and set a course through the waves.

This shows that You can save people from any danger, even allowing those with no experience to travel safely across the waters.

You designed everything with purpose, and as a result, people trust their lives to fragile boats and rafts, yet they make it through stormy seas unharmed.

Long ago, when the proud giants of old were wiped out, the future of the world was saved on a simple wooden ark, and it was Your hand that led humanity forward.

Blessed is the wood that serves a good purpose, but cursed is the idol made by human hands, along with the one who created it.

For an object shaped by human effort should never be called a god.

God hates both wickedness and those who practice it.

He will judge both the act and the person who commits it.

This is why the idols worshiped by nations will face judgment. Even though they are made from materials God created, they have become disgusting, trapping people in lies and leading the foolish astray.

Idolatry was the beginning of sin, and from it, corruption spread into the world.

These false gods were never part of creation from the start, and they will not last forever.

They were made because of human arrogance, and their end is already decided.

For example, a grieving father, heartbroken over the loss of a child, might carve a statue to look like his son or daughter. Over time, he begins to treat this lifeless figure as if it were real, eventually setting up rituals to honor it.

Before long, others follow his example, and the false practice grows into a tradition.

Soon, rulers give orders that these statues should be respected as gods.

When people cannot honor their rulers in person because they live far away, they create statues to represent them. Through these images, they try to show devotion as if the ruler were actually there.

As time passes, even those who never knew the ruler begin to worship the statue. The skill of the artist makes the image look even more impressive, and the people, amazed by its beauty, begin to treat it as a god.

People are deceived into thinking that something man-made has divine power.

But they did not stop there. They drifted even further from the truth,
justifying their foolishness and calling their evil actions "peace."

They went so far as to sacrifice their own children, take part in secret rituals, and engage in wild, uncontrolled celebrations.

They lost all respect for life and marriage, falling into betrayal, adultery, and dishonesty.

The world became filled with violence, murder, theft, deception, corruption, unfaithfulness, chaos, and lies.

People lost their sense of right and wrong. They forgot kindness, had no gratitude, and defiled themselves. Their relationships were ruined by cheating and uncontrolled desires.

The worship of false gods—idols that should never have existed—is the root of all evil, its cause, and its ultimate result.

Those who take part in such worship lose control of themselves. They spread false messages, commit injustice, and have no problem lying under oath.

Since they believe in lifeless statues, they make false promises without fear of consequences.

But their own words and actions will bring punishment upon them.

By worshiping idols, they have insulted God, disrespected His holiness, and led others astray.

It is not the fake gods they swear by that will condemn them,
but their own sins.

God's justice will not fail—He will hold the wicked accountable for everything they have done.

Chapter 15

You, our God, are full of kindness and truth. You are patient and merciful, carefully watching over everything.

Even when we make mistakes, we are still yours because we recognize your authority. Knowing we belong to you gives us the strength to turn away from sin.

To truly understand you is what it means to be righteous, and knowing your power is the key to eternal life.

We have not been fooled by the tricks of people or by the meaningless work of artists who create statues and decorate them with bright colors.

These images may attract the attention of those who lack wisdom, but they are nothing more than lifeless objects with no breath or spirit.

Those who make, desire, and worship such things are chasing after emptiness and will become just as worthless as the idols they honor.

A potter takes soft clay and skillfully shapes it into useful objects.

From the same material, he makes items for both important and ordinary uses, deciding their purpose based on his own choice.

But sometimes, he takes that same clay and creates an idol that has no purpose at all.

This man, who was recently formed from the dust of the earth, will soon return to it when his short life comes to an end. His soul, which was only borrowed, will be taken back.

Yet instead of thinking about how brief his life is, he works anxiously—not because he values his time on earth, but because he wants to compete with goldsmiths, silversmiths, and other craftsmen, showing off his skills in making false gods.

His heart is as worthless as ashes. His hopes are weaker than dust, and his life has even less meaning than the clay he shapes.

This is because he does not know his Creator—the one who gave him life, filled him with a soul, and breathed His spirit into him.

Instead, he treats life as a game and his days as nothing more than an opportunity to gain wealth. He tells himself, **"I must become rich no matter what, even if I have to do wrong."**

Such a man fully understands his sin. He takes fragile clay to make both everyday items and false gods, yet he does not see how pointless his actions are.

Even more foolish and hopeless are those who are enemies of your people—those who have mistreated them.

They bow down to the idols of nations, treating them as gods, even though these statues cannot see, breathe, hear, touch, or walk.

These idols were made by human hands, created by people who themselves rely on the breath of life. No person can make a god.

The craftsmen who build these idols are more valuable than the statues they worship because at least they are alive, while the idols have never had life at all.

Even worse, these people worship the lowest and most meaningless creatures. Compared to other living beings, these are the most foolish and senseless.

They have no beauty that would make anyone admire them. They do not deserve praise and have never received any blessing from God.

Chapter 16

Because of their actions, they were rightfully punished by the very creatures they worshiped, suffering from swarms of insects and vermin.

But in contrast, you blessed your people. You provided them with quail, a rich and satisfying food to meet their hunger.

This happened so that their enemies, desperate for food, would be disgusted by the swarms of pests you sent, losing even the desire to eat. Meanwhile, your people, though they experienced a brief moment of need, were given fine and nourishing food.

It was fair for the oppressors to endure constant suffering, while your people only needed to see the punishment of their enemies.

Even when your people were attacked by wild animals and deadly snakes, your anger did not last long.

You sent these challenges as a warning and gave them a sign of salvation to remind them of your laws.

Those who looked at the sign were not saved by the object itself but by you, the one who rescues all.

Through this, you showed their enemies that only you have the power to save people from danger.

Their enemies were bitten to death by swarms of insects, with no cure for their suffering, because they deserved their punishment.

But your people were protected from the poison of deadly snakes. Your mercy healed them and kept them safe from harm.

They were bitten only as a reminder of your commandments, but you quickly healed them to teach them about your kindness and to prevent them from being ungrateful.

It wasn't herbs or medicine that cured them, but your word, O Lord, which heals all things.

You alone have control over life and death. You lead people to the brink of the grave and bring them back again.

Even when the wicked take life through their evil actions, they cannot return a lost soul or set a captive spirit free.

No one can escape your power.

The ungodly, who refused to recognize you, were struck by your mighty hand. You punished them with strange storms, hail, endless rain, and consuming fire.

In a miraculous way, fire burned even hotter in water—something that should have put it out—proving that creation itself fights to protect the righteous.

At times, the fire was held back so it wouldn't destroy the creatures sent to punish the wicked, allowing them to see that they were under your judgment.

At other times, the fire burned fiercely, even in water, to destroy the crops of an unrighteous land.

But for your people, you provided bread from heaven, food that required no work to prepare. This special bread, which tasted perfect to everyone, satisfied all cravings.

Your kindness was clear in how the bread adjusted to each person's preference, showing your deep care for your children.

Even snow and ice resisted the fire and did not melt, proving that fire destroyed the wicked's crops while burning through hail and flashing through the rain.

But when the fire was needed to help the righteous, it softened its strength and acted with control.

Creation itself, serving you as its Maker, uses its power to punish the wicked while showing kindness to those who trust in you.

At that time, creation changed to serve your people, revealing your endless mercy and care.

This taught your beloved children that it is not food from the earth that truly sustains life, but your word, which protects those who rely on you.

What the fire did not burn melted away with just a gentle ray of sunlight,

Teaching your people to wake early to thank you and to pray as a new day begins.

But the hope of the ungrateful fades like frost in the morning sun, vanishing like water that flows aimlessly and serves no purpose.

Chapter 17

Your judgments are deep and beyond full understanding, and because of this, those without discipline strayed far from the truth.

When lawless people thought they could take control of a holy nation, they found themselves trapped in total darkness. Bound by chains of endless night, they remained hidden inside their homes, cut off from your eternal care.

They thought their secret sins would never be discovered, but instead, they were caught in a heavy cloud of forgetfulness. Fear gripped them, and they were tormented by terrifying visions.

Even the dark places where they tried to hide couldn't protect them from their overwhelming panic. They were surrounded by strange and eerie sounds, and frightening shadows with stern faces appeared before them.

No fire could break through the thick darkness, and not even the brightest stars could light their way.

Instead, a faint, ghostly glow filled them with dread. They became more afraid of the terrifying things their minds imagined than the actual shadows they could see but refused to face.

The magic they once used to mock others was useless now. Their proud claims of wisdom turned into shame and embarrassment.

Those who once bragged about calming troubled minds were now consumed by ridiculous fears.

Even when there was no real danger, they panicked at the sound of insects crawling or the quiet hissing of snakes.

They were frozen in fear, trembling, too scared to even look around, even though the air surrounded them completely.

Wickedness is always cowardly, haunted by its own guilty conscience. The weight of guilt brings fear, making people imagine the worst possible things.

Fear is nothing but the loss of clear thinking.

When reason is thrown away, ignorance takes its place, making the suffering even worse.

As the night covered them like a heavy shadow from the grave, they all suffered the same restless sleep.

They were haunted by terrifying visions, and sudden, unexpected fear took control of them.

No matter what they were doing—standing, lying down, or working—they felt trapped, as if invisible chains were holding them back.

It didn't matter if they were farmers, shepherds, or workers in the wilderness; all of them were consumed by the same overwhelming terror, bound by the heavy chains of darkness.

Even the smallest sounds—wind whispering, birds chirping, water rushing down violently, or stones crashing—filled them with fear.

The quick movements of unseen animals, the growls of wild creatures, or echoes bouncing off mountain caves froze them in place.

While the rest of the world enjoyed bright, clear light and carried on with their daily lives,

They were covered in deep, crushing darkness. It felt like the shadow of eternal night, a warning of what was to come. They felt trapped, as if they were heavier and more weighed down than the darkness itself.

Chapter 18

For your faithful people, you provided a bright and guiding light. Meanwhile, their enemies could hear their voices but couldn't see them. Even though these enemies had harmed them before, they chose not to do so now. Instead, they felt relief that they had also suffered and began to regret the harm they had caused. Some even sought forgiveness.

You gave your people a pillar of fire to lead them on their unknown journey. It acted like a gentle sun during their time of exile, bringing them hope. But the Egyptians, who had imprisoned your children, deserved to be left in the darkness, just as they had tried to keep your people from bringing the light of your law to the world.

After they plotted to destroy the children of the faithful, you saved one abandoned child to expose their guilt. In return, you took their own children and swept away their mighty army in a great flood.

You warned our ancestors about that night ahead of time so they could hold onto your promises and find comfort in their faith. They waited with hope—trusting that the righteous would be saved and that their enemies would be punished. While you brought judgment on their oppressors, you honored your people and brought them closer to you.

Holy children of faithful families made their sacrifices in secret. Together, they entered into the sacred covenant, sharing both the blessings and dangers that came with it. Their ancestors led them in songs of praise. At the same time, cries of grief echoed from their enemies, mourning the children they had lost.

Both slaves and rulers suffered the same punishment, as did the rich and the poor. No one was spared, and countless bodies lay unburied. The living couldn't even bury their dead because, in an instant, their most beloved children had been taken from them.

Even though they had relied on magic and refused to believe in the truth, they were finally forced to admit that the people of God were truly His chosen ones after their firstborn were struck down.

As the earth lay in deep silence and the night reached its darkest point, your powerful word came down from heaven, from your royal throne. Like a fierce warrior, it entered the land that was doomed for destruction, carrying out your sharp command. Death spread everywhere, from the highest places to the lowest.

Terror swept through them. Their dreams filled them with fear, and panic gripped their hearts. They fell to the ground, barely alive, and suddenly realized why they were dying. Their dreams had warned them of what was coming, so they understood exactly why they were suffering.

Even the righteous were touched by death, and many were lost in the wilderness. But your anger did not last long. A pure and faithful man stepped forward to plead for the people. Using prayer and sacred incense as his weapons, he stood between life and death, stopping the disaster and proving his loyalty to you.

He calmed your wrath, not by using physical strength or weapons, but through his words. He reminded you of the promises and oaths you had made to their ancestors, and in doing so, he held back the destroyer. As the dead fell in great numbers, he stepped in and stopped the destruction before it could reach the living.

The robe he wore represented the entire world, and the history of his people was engraved in four rows of precious stones. Your majesty rested upon the crown he wore on his head.

Chapter 19

God's fierce anger struck the wicked without holding back until the very end because He already knew what they would do. Even after letting His people go and urging them to leave, He knew they would soon change their minds and chase after them.

While they were still grieving and crying over their dead, they made another foolish choice. They decided to pursue the very people they had begged to leave and forced out of their land, treating them like runaway slaves.

Their own punishment led them toward their downfall, making them forget the suffering they had already endured. This happened so they could fully experience the justice they deserved and face the consequences of their actions.

Meanwhile, your people traveled on an incredible path, while their enemies met a strange and terrible fate.

All of creation adjusted to follow your commands and protect your people. A cloud covered the camp, providing shelter, and dry land appeared where there had once been water. The Red Sea opened up into a clear road, and a grassy plain rose from the wild waves.

Protected by your hand, your people crossed safely, watching these amazing miracles unfold.

They moved with ease, like horses running through an open field, and leapt like joyful lambs, singing praises to you, O Lord, their Savior.

They remembered the miracles of their journey: how the land, instead of producing livestock, became overrun with swarms of lice, and how the river, instead of fish, was filled with countless frogs.

Later, when they craved rich and satisfying food, they saw a new kind of bird appear. To meet their needs, quails rose from the sea, providing them with nourishment and comfort.

But sinners were not punished without warning. The rumbling thunder had already given them a sign of what was coming. They were justly punished for their cruelty, for they had treated strangers with extreme harshness.

While some simply refuse to welcome outsiders, the Egyptians took it much further—they enslaved the very people who had once helped them. At first, they welcomed their guests with feasts, but later, they forced them into brutal labor, even though they had once lived side by side.

They were also struck with blindness, just like others had been at the doorstep of a righteous man. Trapped in total darkness, they desperately searched for a way out but couldn't even find their own doors.

Just as the strings of a harp create different sounds, the forces of nature changed in amazing ways.

Land animals turned into sea creatures, while those that once swam moved onto dry land. Fire burned fiercely even within water, and water changed its nature to put out flames.

Yet the fire did not harm the creatures walking through it, nor did it melt the delicate grains of heavenly food, which could dissolve so easily.

In every way, O Lord, you showed your power to your people. You honored them, never turning away, and stayed by their side in every place and at every moment.

Thank You for Reading

Dear Reader,

We hope this timeless classic has sparked your imagination and enriched your literary journey. Now that you've turned the final page, we want to share a vision for the future of reading—one where every classic you've ever wanted to explore is at your fingertips, in a format that best suits your life.

We'd like to invite you to gain immediate, unlimited digital & audiobook access to hundreds of the most treasured literary classics ever written—along with the option to secure deluxe paperback, hardcover & box set editions at printing cost. Together, we can spark a new global literary renaissance alongside our small, independent publishing house called "The Library of Alexandria."

Thousands of years ago, the Library of Alexandria stood as a beacon of knowledge—until it was lost to history. We aim to reignite that spirit of preservation and discovery right now, in the modern age—only this time, it's accessible to all, in every language and every format.

Picture a world where every timeless classic, novel, poem, or philosophical treatise is not only available to read but also updated for today's readers—modernized, translated into any language or dialect, and ready to enjoy in any format you choose, whether that is in an eBook, audiobook, paperback, or deluxe hardcover & box set version a printing cost.

By joining our movement to rebuild the modern Library of Alexandria, you become part of an unprecedented mission to offer:

- **Unlimited Audiobook & eBook Access to the Greatest Classics of All Time**

    Instantly explore thousands of legendary works, from Plato and Shakespeare to Jane Austen and Leo Tolstoy. All are instantly ready to read or listen to, giving you a complete literary universe at your fingertips.

- **Paperback & Deluxe Editions at Printing Costs:**

    Purchase any title in a paperback, deluxe hardbound, or deluxe boxset edition at printing costs, shipped right to your doorstep. Curate your personal library of Alexandria with editions worthy of display—crafted to last, designed to captivate, and delivered straight to your door.

- **Modern translations for Contemporary Readers in all languages and dialects**

  Discover a vast selection of classics reimagined in clear, current language—no more struggling with outdated phrases or obscure references. Next to the original versions, we aim to offer translations in as many languages and dialects as possible.

  As we continue our translation efforts and add new languages, readers everywhere can connect with these works as if they were written today. By bridging linguistic divides, you're contributing to ensuring that these timeless stories become more meaningful, accessible, and inspiring for people across the globe.

- **Your Personal Library of Alexandria:**

  Over the months and years, you'll curate a unique physical archive of classics—each volume a testament to your taste, curiosity, and love of knowledge. It's not just about owning books—it's about curating a cultural legacy you'll cherish and pass down for generations to come.

- **Join a Global Literary Renaissance:**

  Your support fuels an ongoing mission: allowing us to reinvest in offering deluxe print editions (including special boxsets) at their true cost, broaden the range of available formats and translations, and extend the reach of these works to new audiences worldwide. By joining today, you're not just preserving a legacy of masterpieces; you set in motion a powerful wave of literary accessibility.

We are more than a publisher—we're a movement, and we can't do it alone. Your support lets us scale our mission, preserving and reimagining history's greatest works for tomorrow's readers.

Become a Torchbearer of knowledge.

Thank you for picking up this book and allowing us into your literary journey. As you turn the pages, know that you're part of something larger: a global effort to keep these stories alive, share their wisdom across borders and generations, and spark a true cultural revival for the modern era.

If this resonates with you—please consider taking the next step by visiting:

www.libraryofalexandria.com

With gratitude and a shared love of knowledge,

The Modern Library of Alexandria Team

Visit:

www.libraryofalexandria.com

Or scan the code below:

www.ingramcontent.com/pod-product-compliance
Lightning Source LLC
LaVergne TN
LVHW030631080426
835512LV00021B/3451